SPELLING

1

SPELLING

by John Smith

1

CASSELL

Cassell plc.
Wellington House
125 Strand
London WC2R 0BB

Reprinted 1988, 1989, 1990, 1991, 1992, 1993, 1995

ISBN 0 304 31280 0

Typeset by Kalligraphics Ltd, Surrey

Printed and bound by
Hollen Street Press, Berwick upon Tweed

For Teachers and Parents

1. These books are designed to give children practice in spelling once or twice a day – when they come in from play, for instance.
2. Used only once a day, a child will go through this book five times and write 3,000 spellings in 'families' in the course of a school year.
3. Each page is a challenge to a child, as a crossword puzzle is to an adult, and should be presented in that light.
4. Correct spelling is all-important. The accurate writing of the answers is the main reason for doing the page; the solving of the clues is of secondary importance. An answer which is incorrectly spelt should be marked wrong.
5. If this book is used in the few minutes after play, scarcely any teaching time is taken up, and lessons begin quickly, quietly and purposefully.

For Girls and Boys

1. Number your page 1 to 15.
2. Read the clue; choose the word from the 'frame' which best fits the clue, and write it against the proper number.
3. Where two 'frame' words appear to fit the same clue, careful thought will show you that one of them is better than the other.
4. Only correctly spelt answers will be counted.

Contents

1. A train runs on this
2. Luggage is put on this in a bus or train
3. A heavy blow
4. Hikers often carry one on their backs
5. Potatoes are put in this
6. It is always nice to get — home
7. Loose, not tight

ack

back
pack
slack
rack
whack
track
sack

8. They work in the kitchen
9. A place with lots of trees
10. Not bad
11. At the end of your leg
12. You read it
13. We must — at the blackboard
14. For hanging things on
15. Trembled

oo

book
cooks
wood
shook
hook
good
foot
look

1. Sailors walk on it
2. Birds do this
3. A sunken ship
4. A part of the body
5. Something very tiny

eck

peck
deck
wreck
speck
neck

6. Next — I shall be in a new class
7. Strict
8. To put the food on the plates
9. A sharp pull
10. She ate — dinner

er

jerk
serve
term
her
stern

11. Do you — in fairies?
12. May I have a — of chocolate?
13. A word meaning the leader
14. A farmer put his animals into this
15. Someone who steals

ie

chief
field
piece
thief
believe

1. Fast

2. The sound a clock makes

3. He was using a walking —

4. You do this to a football

5. Please — me a flower

6. A baby hen

7. You do this to a lollipop

ick

- stick
- pick
- chick
- lick
- kick
- quick
- tick

8. Put it in the soil and it grows

9. We will — the ducks

10. We put shoes on them

11. An animal

12. A part of the face

13. Seven days

14. We do this when our team wins

15. It's found in a bed

ee

- sheet
- week
- seed
- feed
- feet
- cheek
- deer
- cheer

1. A very large stone
2. Kerry lives in the next — of flats
3. A — of sheep were in the field
4. Please — the door
5. Worn on the foot
6. The car crash gave us a —
7. Tells us the time

ock

sock
lock
rock
shock
clock
block
flock

8. Dogs do this
9. Something to eat
10. A part of the body
11. It is fun to go to a birthday —
12. A fierce fish
13. Begin
14. Soldiers are in the —
15. A word meaning a piece

ar

part
tart
bark
army
arm
party
start
shark

1. You do this to a sweet
2. A bird
3. The tower was — by lightning
4. A big lorry
5. Father said 'Good-bye' and wished Tim good —

uck

truck
suck
duck
luck
struck

6. They all put on — coats
7. You may take — this one or that one
8. You may take — this one nor that one
9. Thin tubes in our bodies for carrying the blood
10. 4×2

ei

eight
their
either
veins
neither

11. To hold a ball when it is thrown to you
12. A word meaning to bring
13. For lighting a fire
14. It tells us the time
15. Made with a needle and thread

tch

match
stitch
watch
catch
fetch

1. Hit this with a hammer
2. A pig has a curly one
3. An engine and coaches
4. Ships — to other lands
5. Ask him to — at the car
6. Arif got wet in the —
7. We think with our —

8. 10×3
9. Owls, robins and sparrows
10. Spin round
11. Daniel put on a clean —
12. It comes before 'second'
13. You should not eat with — hands
14. Boys and —
15. Does not wobble

ai

sail
brain
nail
tail
rain
wait
train

ir

birds
firm
dirty
thirty
girls
shirt
first
whirl

ing

1. Going fast
2. Sometimes he wears a crown
3. A bird has two of these
4. Wasps and bees can —
5. Wear it on your finger
6. The — broke and the kite flew away
7. We — songs

sing
wings
string
king
running
ring
sting

or

8. It was a thunder —
9. Knife, — and spoon
10. She — up the paper
11. The part of an apple we don't eat
12. Painful
13. Ships sail into these
14. He is learning to play an —
15. What — of pen would you like?

ports
storm
core
sort
sore
organ
fork
tore

1. We wear this
2. Breakfast cereal
3. We score these in football and netball
4. To stay on the top of the water
5. Another name for a ship
6. A groan
7. A wide ditch which used to go round a castle

oa

goals
boat
oats
moan
moat
coat
float

8. If you play with fire you may be —
9. A cat does this
10. To move round
11. Hangs at the windows
12. We keep money in this
13. A large bird
14. It keeps some animals warm
15. They care for us in hospital

ur

purrs
fur
burnt
turkey
turn
curtain
nurses
purse

1. Put this on your bicycle to make it go easily
2. Money
3. To make water very hot
4. To fasten together
5. Plants grow in —
6. A snake can — itself up
7. The motor-bike made a loud —

oi

boil
soil
oil
coins
noise
join
coil

8. It comes out of a hot kettle
9. Not strong
10. There are 11 players in a football —
11. A bird has one of these
12. To take something which is not yours
13. We enjoy three good ones each day
14. I — with my ear
15. To be afraid

ea

beak
steal
fear
weak
meals
hear
steam
team

ss

1. 'I'm wearing my new —,' whispered Tanya
2. The sound a snake makes
3. Please — the salt
4. Don't make a — about it
5. A game played on a board
6. How many children are there in your —?
7. To push hard

press
chess
hiss
dress
pass
fuss
class

ou

8. A building
9. An animal
10. The boy is — ten years old
11. Not in
12. Fat people are often said to be —
13. To push out the lips and sulk
14. If you grind wheat you get this
15. To call out loudly

out
shout
flour
house
mouse
stout
about
pout

1. Used with a needle
2. The sound cups and saucers make
3. Nice to look at
4. Bigger and rounder
5. To throw all over the place
6. To speak in a low voice
7. Adam's brakes stopped him from — the wall

tt

hitting
scatter
clatter
pretty
mutter
fatter
cotton

8. To wrinkle up the brows
9. He slid — the stairs
10. A wolf — in the night
11. We'll drive into — today
12. A short fall of rain
13. A pretty plant
14. A bird said to be wise
15. The clock in the church — struck five

ow

owl
flower
down
tower
frown
town
howls
shower

1. A road
2. Sticky stuff
3. The Union Jack is red, white and —
4. A story that really happened is a — one
5. It comes after Monday

ue

true
blue
glue
Tuesday
avenue

6. For carrying things on
7. It comes after Saturday
8. Give money to someone
9. To say one's prayers
10. A soft material used to make models

ay

pay
tray
clay
Sunday
pray

11. A dark patch on the skin
12. You can drink the — of an orange
13. Apples, oranges and grapes are different kinds of —
14. Often eaten with a cup of tea
15. Something to wear

ui

suit
fruit
bruise
juice
biscuit

Days

1. It comes after Wednesday
2. The day after Friday
3. On Mondays we call it 'tomorrow'
4. The day before Tuesday
5. The day before Thursday

Tuesday
Saturday
Wednesday
Thursday
Monday

oy

6. Father Christmas seems to bring lots of these
7. To tease
8. Happiness
9. Not a girl but a —
10. To have a good time

boy
toys
annoy
joy
enjoy

ey

11. Our new video cost a lot of —
12. At the seaside I had a — ride
13. This animal lives in the trees
14. Put this in a lock
15. Bees make this food

key
honey
donkey
money
monkey

1. A colour

2. Used for firing arrows

3. Not quick

4. A bow and —

5. A bird

6. To become bigger

7. It's white, soft and fun to play in

ow

bow
snow
grow
crow
slow
arrow
yellow

8. Fighting between armies

9. To clean with water

10. A large, graceful bird

11. Like a bee and stings

12. I did not know I — late

13. Used for telling the time

14. Vicky — a bike for Christmas

15. Something to drink

wa

was
wasp
war
water
wash
swan
watch
wants

1. Something we eat at tea-time
2. A tiger is wild, but a dog is —
3. We eat our food from this
4. There's a speedboat on the —
5. A thin stick
6. A garden tool
7. Another name for a story

e

lake
cake
rake
cane
plate
tale
tame

8. Many children are good at — their sweets with others
9. Having a bath
10. The thunder kept — us up
11. Making a wild animal less wild
12. Trembling
13. The twins went roller — today
14. Cooking
15. Using a rake

ing

baking
raking
skating
sharing
taming
bathing
waking
shaking

1. To travel on a horse is to — it
2. Frozen water
3. To go down head first
4. Our backbone
5. Amanda is learning to — a car
6. To keep out of sight
7. A heap

e

ride
spine
hide
dive
ice
pile
drive

8. Keeping out of sight
9. Made of sugar
10. Travelling on horseback
11. We eat our dinner in the — room
12. Amanda has passed her — test
13. Drying with a cloth
14. Going head first into water
15. Putting in heaps

ing

dining
riding
hiding
diving
icing
piling
driving
wiping

1. Things we wear
2. A short way of saying 'telephone'
3. A long rounded piece of wood or metal
4. To sleep lightly
5. Lee broke a — in his wrist
6. A pebble
7. It makes you laugh

e

bone
doze
stone
joke
clothes
phone
pole

8. Throwing stones
9. Making jokes
10. Grandad was — among the leaves with his stick
11. Dull and not interesting
12. In the bus it said 'No —'
13. A short way of saying 'telephoning'
14. Having a light sleep
15. Putting things away until later

ing

poking
dozing
stoning
joking
smoking
boring
phoning
storing

1. Toothpaste is sold in a —
2. The doctor found a — for the disease
3. We are taught to — tools
4. A month
5. A dried plum

e

June
tube
cure
prune
use

6. Sometimes made of rubber
7. Dr. Brown is — the lad of his spots
8. Mrs. Jones is — her red umbrella
9. They were busy — the roses
10. A string broke as he was — his violin

ing

using
tubing
pruning
tuning
curing

11. Not on
12. The teachers at a school
13. A sticky sweet
14. A drink
15. Does not bend

ff

toffee
coffee
stiff
staff
off

1. In the play the — wears a crown
2. ¼
3. Fast
4. Not noisy
5. He told her that Christopher was — a clever boy

qu

quick
quite
queen
quarter
quiet

6. Tracey — the song well
7. Very cross
8. A loud noise
9. Dominic walked to the door and — the bell
10. Be helpful and always — up your coat

ang

bang
sang
hang
rang
angry

11. Having a lot of money
12. A boy's name
13. A garden of fruit trees
14. It is good to have — a kind friend
15. Your writing is — better

ch

much
such
rich
Richard
orchard

Numbers

1. 7−6
2. 8÷4
3. 9÷3
4. 2×2
5. Half a dozen
6. 2+3
7. 4+3

two
four
seven
one
five
six
three

aw

8. To make a picture with a pencil
9. A part of the face
10. A dog's foot
11. Not cooked
12. A tool for cutting wood
13. Animals sleep on it
14. Babies — before they walk
15. Parking on double yellow lines is against the —

paw
saw
draw
law
crawl
jaw
raw
straw

mm

1. We like to fill this with food
2. Only a baby would suck this
3. Another name for Mum
4. After the Spring comes the —
5. A tool
6. He plays a drum
7. Shut with a bang

Summer
Mummy
dummy
slammed
drummer
hammer
tummy

nn

8. If Mark came first he was the —
9. If you don't eat you will grow —
10. A meal
11. Fastened with a pin
12. Faster than walking
13. Sly
14. For — a prize his aunt gave him a book token
15. Tom — all over his face

pinned
grinned
running
cunning
winning
winner
dinner
thinner

ea

1. Near the sea
2. At the table we should have — hands
3. I would love to be in the netball —
4. Pork, beef and lamb
5. Something to sit on
6. Last night I had a —
7. In a sale things are often —

meat
seat
dream
team
cheaper
beach
clean

ing

8. The soldiers were — past us
9. They were — strawberries
10. Jane is — to Ireland today
11. The children were — a ball
12. They are — me a letter
13. Granny was — Emma's hair
14. His tooth was —
15. The baby wouldn't stop —

aching
marching
cutting
picking
writing
flying
crying
kicking

1. A horse's home
2. Another name for a violin
3. We sit at one for meals
4. Poor, untidy writing
5. Joins the leg to the foot
6. A small dirty pool
7. The centre

le

scribble
ankle
table
stable
middle
fiddle
puddle

8. I helped to — the dinner
9. Seven days
10. We hang our coats on this
11. Something to read
12. They — hands
13. Carried by a shepherd
14. This is like an onion
15. We must — before we cross the road

k

book
look
week
cook
hook
shook
crook
leek

1. A flower
2. A fruit
3. A tiny child
4. A book you write in
5. A woman
6. Often at the top of a Christmas tree
7. He helped to — the shopping

y

fairy
carry
daisy
baby
diary
berry
lady

8. A sharp tool
9. He rode on horseback
10. Hit
11. You tie this
12. Kim — all her tables
13. To go down on the knees
14. A part of the body
15. Mum — with two needles

kn

knee
knew
knits
knock
knight
knife
kneel
knot

1. Natalie often — the shopping
2. Tiny children
3. Fruits
4. Flowers
5. These are supposed to live in 'Fairyland'
6. Women
7. Books in which we write what happens

ies

fairies
carries
daisies
babies
diaries
ladies
berries

8. I got six sums right and one —
9. A tool for picking up lumps
10. Not weak
11. A shape like this 
12. The rabbit was found — the flowers
13. A blackbird's — is very beautiful
14. How — have you lived here?
15. When hit it makes a noise

ong

song
long
wrong
tongs
gong
strong
oblong
among

1. A candle is made of this
2. 6
3. 16
4. 60
5. For putting things in
6. Animals with red fur and bushy tails
7. A tool for chopping wood

x

six
axe
boxes
sixteen
sixty
wax
foxes

8. Frozen rain
9. Engines run on iron —
10. The postman brings the —
11. I like to — pictures
12. The dog lifted up its paw in —
13. Links of metal
14. The tea made a bad — on the cloth
15. The water from the sink runs into the —

ai

pain
drain
rails
stain
paint
hail
chain
mail

1. A fruit
2. A meal at night
3. He is very — at his new school
4. We — at the red light
5. Mum — her basket in surprise
6. A metal
7. These are worn on the feet

pp

happy
apple
supper
slippers
copper
dropped
stopped

8. Not alive
9. The air we breathe out is our —
10. At six we heard the — forecast
11. A food made from flour
12. Scott put his cap on his —
13. The teacher — us a story
14. He can't hear you because he is —
15. A heavy metal

ea

head
bread
deaf
dead
breath
lead
read
weather

1. We climb these
2. Hair of a light colour is said to be —
3. We breathe this
4. For sitting on
5. I'm wearing a new — of shoes
6. It grows on our heads
7. Please can you — my bike?

air

hair
air
fair
pair
stairs
chair
repair

8. Everyone
9. Tumble
10. The — was packed for the meeting
11. Built of bricks and mortar
12. I'll — for you after tea
13. This market — sells skipping ropes
14. It is round and used in games
15. High

all

tall
stall
ball
all
wall
hall
call
fall

age

1. Smaller than a town
2. Words are printed on this
3. Money paid to you at the end of a week
4. To be in a bad temper is to be in a —
5. A corridor
6. Nigel is six years of —
7. Actors act on this

rage
wage
page
stage
village
passage
age

Numbers

8. 4×2
9. 2×5
10. 3×5
11. 3×3
12. 7+4
13. A dozen
14. 2×7
15. 15−2

ten
thirteen
twelve
fourteen
nine
eight
fifteen
eleven

1. He wears a uniform
2. The middle
3. The Queen lives in a —
4. Small animals
5. A very large town
6. Where films are shown
7. A ring

c

palace
city
policeman
centre
circle
mice
cinema

8. Cars drive along this
9. I like — potatoes
10. To put in water
11. My — feels sore today
12. It is burnt on fires
13. A baby horse
14. Used in a rowing boat
15. He bought a — of bread

oa

coal
road
roast
soak
oars
loaf
foal
throat

ied

1. Martin — when his dog was lost
2. Cooked in a frying pan
3. Salma — hard with her reading
4. Did not live
5. Did not tell the truth

tried
fried
cried
lied
died

le

6. We need a — of tomato sauce
7. Small
8. A baby's plaything
9. A funny little laugh
10. A hedgehog has many sharp —
11. Open the door with this
12. A mark on the face
13. Used for boiling water
14. He was very — with the kitten
15. Guns carried by soldiers

giggle
freckle
little
handle
prickles
gentle
bottle
rifles
kettle
rattle

rr

borrow
sparrows
worry
carried
mirror
arrows
carrot

1. A vegetable
2. They shoot — from bows
3. May I — your knife, please?
4. Small birds
5. Don't — about it, David
6. Pat saw herself in the —
7. I — it down to the beach

Buildings

office
house
hotel
station
hospital
school
garage
church

8. A building for a car
9. Papers and typewriters are found here
10. A place to stay on our holidays perhaps
11. A building for prayer
12. A place where we learn our lessons
13. Sick people often go here
14. The building we live in
15. Trains stop at this

ace

face
ace
trace
lace
race
place
pace

1. Used to tie your shoe
2. To go fast
3. A step or stride
4. To go over the lines with a pencil
5. Show me the — where it hurts
6. The front part of the head
7. The 'one' in a pack of cards

bb

rubber
rabbits
rubbing
bubbles
cabbage
pebble
wobble
nibbled

8. A vegetable
9. If you — on a bicycle you may fall off
10. Small children blow these
11. A small stone on the beach
12. They make lovely pets
13. Jason's new rabbit — at the carrot
14. Used for taking out pencil marks
15. The girl was — her sore knee

1. Turn to the left not to the —
2. The dark hours
3. A battle
4. His shoes hurt because they were too —
5. The trees and lakes were a lovely —
6. At night we switch on the —
7. It — snow on Christmas Day

ight

fight
light
night
sight
might
right
tight

8. A yellow bird which sings well
9. A fish
10. A young cat
11. A big bird which often talks
12. This lives in a hutch
13. A small horse
14. Young dogs
15. A small animal with a long tail

Pets

rabbit
kitten
canary
goldfish
parrot
mouse
puppies
pony

1. Went on sleeping
2. Henry — his computer locked in a cupboard
3. I — quietly upstairs to bed
4. Cried
5. Used a sweeping brush

ept

wept
slept
kept
crept
swept

6. Every car has a — to hold the petrol
7. I want to — you very much
8. A long piece of flat wood
9. It looks after our money
10. Munir goes to the skating —
11. I — it will be a fine day
12. A colour
13. The ship — to the bottom of the sea
14. A part of a chain
15. To move the eyelids

nk

rink
bank
pink
sank
blink
thank
tank
plank
think
link

The Body

1. We have eight of these and two thumbs
2. A joint in the arm
3. A joint halfway down the leg
4. The part of the body where the brain is
5. A part of the finger
6. Hairs just above the eyes
7. Used for listening
8. Used for seeing
9. This grows on the head
10. The tongue and the teeth are in this
11. Used for swallowing
12. This joins the hand and the arm
13. Where the arm joins the body
14. We have one on each hand
15. This joint helps us to move our foot

eyes
ears
mouth
fingers
elbow
throat
hair
knee
eyebrows
wrist
knuckle
ankle
shoulder
head
thumb

1. A milk pudding
2. Animals
3. Kate has been to a very — party
4. A piece of cake
5. Shaped like sugar-lumps and used in games
6. Two times
7. Frozen water

ice

twice
rice
ice
mice
slice
dice
nice

8. A looking glass
9. A seaman
10. Used for shaving
11. The — school has a big hall
12. If we are very ill we send for a —
13. A person who acts
14. The chief person in a town
15. Their — car broke down

or

actor
doctor
motor
mirror
sailor
razor
junior
mayor

wh

1. A huge sea-creature
2. The colour of snow
3. A lion-trainer may use one
4. To talk very softly
5. A car always has a spare one
6. You blow this
7. A word often used when asking questions

whip
which
whisper
wheel
whale
white
whistle

str

8. Not crooked
9. As — as a horse
10. A fruit
11. To walk with big paces
12. A road in a town
13. We love to — the kittens
14. Stern
15. Someone we don't know

street
stranger
stride
strong
stroke
straight
strict
strawberry

1. A very small bird
2. To put words on paper
3. We must — the birthday present
4. A part of the arm
5. A sunken ship

wr

wrap
wren
write
wreck
wrist

6. Something we wear
7. This grows in a garden
8. He tripped on the — of the pavement
9. An animal
10. A small shelf

dge

edge
badge
ledge
hedge
badger

11. Used for tidying the hair
12. To go up higher
13. A — person cannot talk
14. Often left on a plate
15. A young sheep

mb

dumb
comb
crumb
lamb
climb

The Year

1. The first month of the year
2. second
3. third
4. fourth
5. fifth
6. sixth
7. seventh
8. eighth
9. ninth
10. tenth
11. eleventh
12. twelfth
13. Fifty-two — make a year
14. Twelve — make a year
15. A — year has one extra day

April
May
August
January
leap
March
weeks
February
September
July
December
June
months
October
November